Jade's party

Story written by Gill Munton
Illustrated by Tim Archbold

Speed Sounds

Consonants   *Ask children to say the sounds.*

f	l	m	n	r	s	v	z	sh	th	ng
ff	ll	mm	nn	rr	ss	**(ve)**	zz			nk
ph	le	mb	kn	wr	se		se			
					ce		s			

b	c	d	g	h	j	p	qu	t	w	x	y	ch
bb	k	dd	gg		j	pp		tt	**(wh)**			tch
	ck				ge							

Each box contains one sound but sometimes more than one grapheme.
*Focus graphemes for this story are **circled**.*

Vowels

Ask children to say the sounds in and out of order.

a	e	i	o	u	**ay**	ee	igh	ow
	ea				**a-e**	ea	i-e	o-e
					a	y	ie	o
						e	i	
at	hen	in	on	up	day	see	high	blow

oo	oo	ar	or	air	ir	ou	oy
u-e			oor	are	ur		oi
ue			ore		er		
zoo	look	car	for	fair	whirl	shout	boy

5

Story Green Words

Ask children to read the words first in Fred Talk and then say the word.

Jade　cake　group　stale　pale　blame　shame

Ask children to say the syllables and then read the whole word.

choc|o|late　lem|on|ade　teen|age　troll|ey　curr|ant　be|have

pave|ment　fish|cake　spark|lers　mu|sic*

Ask children to read the root first and then the whole word with the suffix.

shop → shopping　plate → plates　race → raced

* Challenge Words

6

Vocabulary Check

Discuss the meaning (as used in the story) after the children have read each word.

	definition:	sentence:
group	*a pop group*	*... we got a good one by a new group.*
raced	*walked really quickly*	*We raced along to the bus stop.*
stale	*food that isn't fresh*	*Out of the bag came a packet of stale fishcakes ...*
past the sell-by date	*food that is stale*	*(past the sell-by date).*
sparklers	*metal sticks with special material that lights up and sparkles when lit*	*I had a chocolate cake with seven sparklers on it.*

Red Words

brother	all	where	said
one	was	you	of
any	son	over	does
school	once	school	there
who	are	your	watch

Jade's party

My name is Jade.

It was my birthday on Sunday,
and I had a party.

But the party almost didn't happen!

I'll tell you why.

Dad made a shopping list.

twenty bread rolls

three packets of cheese

ten bags of crisps

ten milk shakes

ten cans of lemonade

a packet of napkins and a packet of plates

a packet of balloons

a CD of party music

a big chocolate cake

Dave's my teenage brother.
Dad asked him to take me to
the shops on the bus to get all
the stuff for the party.

We got a trolley, and Dave looked
at the list.

First, we went to the place where they bake bread.
Dave picked up twenty rolls and put them in the trolley.
(I picked up a currant bun, and hid it under the rolls.)

Then I found the cheese.
(Dave found the currant bun,
and told me to behave.)

Crisps ...
milk shakes ...
lemonade ...

The trolley was filling up.

Party napkins, plates and a big packet of balloons.
Dave said he'd blow them up.

A CD – we got a good one by a new group.

And then the most important thing:
a chocolate cake (the biggest, with 'Happy Birthday' on top).

We went to the checkout to pay. A girl put all the
stuff in plastic bags and gave them to Dave.

Then we raced along the pavement to the bus stop.
We made up party games on the way.

Dad started to unpack the shopping.

Out came ... a packet of stale fishcakes

(past the sell-by date) ...

shampoo ... a cabbage ...

a can of hair spray ... a bunch of grapes ...

a jar of marmalade ... and a jumbo pack of nappies!

Dad's face went pale.

"For goodness' sake, Dave!" he said. "What have you got to say?"

Dave said, "We must have picked up the wrong shopping by mistake.

Plastic bags all look the same to me. I'll take the blame, Dad.

I'll take it all back to the shops on Monday."

Well, it was a bit of a shame.

I hate grapes, and we didn't need hair spray – or nappies!

But it was okay in the end.

We had the party at a pizza place instead.

We had pizza, and chips, and pop.

Then, out came a man with a birthday cake!

A chocolate one, with seven sparklers on it. For me!

Questions to talk about

Ask children to TTYP each question using 'Fastest finger' (FF) or 'Have a think' (HaT).

p.9 (FF) How did Jade celebrate her birthday on Sunday?

p.10 (HaT) What do you think is the most important thing on the list?

p.11 (FF) What did they pick up first?

(HaT) Why did Jade hide the currant bun?

p.12 (FF) What did Dave say when he found the currant bun?

p.13 (FF) Who put all the stuff into plastic bags?

p.14 (HaT) Why did Dad's face turn pale when he started to unpack the shopping?

p.15 (FF) Where did they have the party instead?

Questions to read and answer

(Children complete without your help.)

1. How many packets of cheese did Dad ask them to get?

2. Who took Jade shopping?

3. Why did Jade and Dave race along the pavement to the bus stop?

4. Why was Dad cross?

5. Why was it OK at the end?

Speedy Green Words

Ask children to practise reading the words across the rows, down the columns and in and out of order clearly and quickly.

name	made	why	take
mistake	same	place	instead
name	started	birthday	party
looked	first	milk	important
happy	goodness	have	girl